Hazen Desmond Walker

WALKER'S WISE WORDS

to

Friends, Family & Strangers

Copyright 2023 @ Hazen Desmond Walker

All rights reserved. No part of this publication may be reproduced, distributed or transmitted in any form or by any means, including photocopying, recording or other electronic or mechanical methods, without the prior written permission of the publisher, except in case of brief quotations embodied in reviews and other non-commercial uses permitted by copyright law. Permission requests can be emailed to the publisher as listed below.

Published in the United States by Hazen Desmond Walker
Memphis, TN
Hazendesmond@gmail.com

Edited by Marvin Mims Sr.
Boldtn04@yahoo.com

Illustrated by Creative Next
thecreativenext@gmail.com

Formatted by Nonon Tech & Design

Names: Hazen Desmond Walker, Author | Mims Sr., Marvin, Editor

Title: Walker's Wise Words

Description: Memphis, TN, self-published by Hazen Desmond Walker

Subjects: United States | Family | African-American Families

ISBN: 979-8-218-34037-7

Cover designed by Joshua Desmond Walker, walker.joshua73@yahoo.com

I dedicate this book to my Papa, Nene, Mom and Dad.

FOREWORD

My name is Marvin Mims Sr., and I am the grandfather of Hazen Desmond Walker who is 10 years of age. He is the first-born grandson of Anita and myself. We have had the pleasure of helping raise and nurture this blessed young man. Hazen has a love for the Lord, family, and friends. Hazen is an awesome big brother to his baby brother Addison. They both enjoy loving each other and wrestling with each other. Hazen is a self-professed architect and will pursue his dreams further when he graduates from High School. Hazen parents Joshua Walker and Tracy Ann Walker have developed him into a caring young man who is bold in lifting others in prayer. I affectionately call him "My Prayer Man." Hazen has a unique way of talking with God simply both intellectually and spiritually at the same time. His creativity in building Lego designs is truly unique. Hazen is a self-determined young man and when he starts a project is committed to completing it, especially when it comes to assembling Lego sets.

Hazen is adored by his Memphis, TN family, Houston, TX family, and his St. Mark Baptist Church family where he accepted Christ as His personal Savior and was baptized. Hazen is a dedicated writer, and, in this book, he shares words of wisdom designed to enrich the reader's life.

Thanking God for Hazen,
Papa

INTRODUCTION

My story: "Walker's Wise Words" is about the things Jesus tells us to do. I have learned many wise words from reading my bible. I am reminding you about God's word with my wise sayings. I have conversations with different characters throughout my book giving them suggestions for life. I hope my book will inspire readers to walk in wisdom. I believe you will enjoy this book!

Sincerely,
Hazen

The End

www.ingramcontent.com/pod-product-compliance
Lightning Source LLC
Chambersburg PA
CBHW061350010526
44107CB00011B/890